To Maeve,
In gratitude for all
she has done for our family
down through the years.
You were the kindest And most generous
of friends.   Michael.

September 1st, 2019.

f i f t y

p o e m s

m i c h a e l

g o r m a n

Michael Gorman

Books of *taste* Created with *passion* In the heart of *Connemara*

w w w . a r t i s a n h o u s e . i e

Reverie, 1998, Joe Boske.

'Once in a blue moon, a book appears that changes the way you think. *Fifty Poems* is just such a book. A work thronged with characters who shoulder their way into memory – people living in fear; people facing death; people rejoicing in love. This is the story of our lives, our Pyrrhic victories and our silent, almost unnoticed losses. Michael Gorman's poems stand shoulder to shoulder with Kavanagh, Durcan, and O'Driscoll in a beautiful, heartbreaking, and heart-warming book.'

John MacKenna

In Michael Gorman's new book we are asked to consider the unconsidered – those who are sidelined by history, those who have been betrayed by the Republic, those who never got a look in, emigrants out of Ireland, and immigrants into Ireland, struggling for a place to call home. A profound act of compassion, this book teems with life – sensitive portraits of the actual living, memorials to the ghosts of those who gave life and meaning to the poet in his formation. Gratitude for the instructing universe is a key element, as is a wicked and pointed sense of the absurd. Many poems are brief and exquisite dramas snatched from the flow – Gorman's impeccable eye and ear can sketch a life in a phrase. Love letters to family and friends, in keen awareness of our brief spell in history, give the work heft, gravitas, and grace.

When Michael Gorman and I were starting out on our paths, John McGahern described him to me as 'one of the best minds of your generation'. 'Go talk to him,' he said. I have always been thankful that I did. Our enduring conversation, like this collection, has been salvific and a blessing.

Paula Meehan

'One by one these bright poem-pennies fuse in your fist to reveal, when opened, a sun-gold gleaming sovereign. Not only lyrical and acute but, more importantly, consistently sincere and true. Marvellous.'

Patrick McCabe

🔊 A reading of this poem by Michael Gorman is available to download or listen to on *www.artisanhouse.ie/michaelgorman*

To speak in a flat voice
Is all that I can do.

James Wright, from 'Speak',
in *Shall We Gather at the River*
(Wesleyan University Press, 1967).

Early on, in school, we learned of the
Fianna and of the day young Oisín fell
from his horse and became an old man
before he hit the ground. Sometimes the
fable is truer than life itself. When I fell
from a horse I tried to, but could not,
retrieve images that were dear to me.
They are gathered here in fifty poems,
half new and half collected. I offer them
in memory of our sister, Paula. The Sligo
in the poems was, in a committed way,
far more hers than it was ever mine.

Michael Gorman, 2019.

The Rattle

When the troponin proteins were released
and I could go no further,
stuck under the windmill farm
on the Spiddal–Moycullen road,
what was I carrying?

The heat from red brick in the evenings.
The louder noises of near-empty trains.
The old man who stopped me as a child,
looking for directions to the County Home,
his belongings covered in brown paper
tied with rough twine.
The parallel strips of dust
gathered in the folds of sheets
left hanging on the line overnight
when we lived at Ducane Road.
The cries of seagulls
following a chef's white bucket
as he emptied fish heads
back into the sea
at Inishbofin.

None of these things,
nothing I ever saw or heard.
Only a cold loneliness
moving out of reach,
a constricted affection
for the passing world.

Blast

From Sleepy Hollow
to the Deepwater Quay,
I'll take bloody good care
you won't forget them.

The woman calling meal numbers
in the pub beside the river.
The man you stood behind
in Brennan's Drapery Store
buying a new suit of clothes
to bury his dead son in.

The girl shouting late at night
across the walls of Wormwood Scrubs,
'Are you there, Glasgow?
Are you there, wee Jock?'
The row of Normandy poplars
coming into East Acton.
The row of golf-range cubicles
facing the sea at Salthill.
The black and white dog at Moormead
racing late trains from the park,
the upright red poles on the platform
strong in the growing dark.

I . C . U .

Lying there at our mercy,
you're getting all the news
whether you like it or not.
The home place is so quiet now,
we can hear a car change gear
from a mile across the fields.
Can you remember the flapping
of pigeons' wings early in the morning
on railway platforms, the shudder
in the launderette before the machine's
final spin?
It was Cockburn's turn today.
The Albanians ran along Brindisi pier
faster than children in any playground.
In Omaha, Nebraska, a man is selling his eye
for 10,000 dollars.
You were right about most things.
Eaten bread is soon forgotten.
Money refuses to grow on trees.
But the man who made time
did not make plenty of it,
least not enough for you and me, Joey,
not near enough for us.

Heroes

Kerchief and whiskers.
Flushed and flustered
from all the shouting,
Ned Kelly, the last town crier,
was ringing a golden bell
with a blue wooden handle,
reeling off the attractions
of the Aughamore Regatta.

Holding a small mirror
in his left hand,
shooting a gun over his shoulder
with the right,
Kit Carson knocked a cigarette
clean from his assistant's mouth
across the lit-up stage
of the packed Gillooly Hall.

Jimmy Hasty, the one-armed man,
was playing for Dundalk.
He had vertical take-off.
From a standing start
he rose higher than any.
His movements were tidy
and his feet were quick.

At the final whistle
we ran on to the pitch
to get a closer look.
The left sleeve of his jersey
was tied in a knot
just under the stump.

The Month of May

Standing over my mother's dead body,
I note, as for the first time,
the freckles on her neck and shoulder
gone from the world of small gesture
that never drew attention to itself,
the way she sprinkled a modicum of salt
along the edge of a closed egg salad sandwich,
years before, in the Mozart café.

Everything outside is suddenly magnified;
I can follow individual blades of grass
moving on the hospital lawn,
a poster on a faraway pole
in familiar blocks of colour
declares the circus is in town.
Alex Lacey, lion-tamer, the Flying Sousas
acrobatic troupe, Miss Beatrix Spindler
with her amazing Spanish horses
are appearing at Sligo Fairgreen.

She carted us off together, once,
paid in to an everyday field
beside the river at Ballisodare
where we watched stars of all-in wrestling
avoid each other entirely
as they crashed into parallel ropes
on a makeshift, elevated stage.

We never look closely enough.
After the show was over,
the cars filed out an open gate,
midges hovered in the riverlight.

Letterfrack

'Oh. Mammy, Mammy, Mammy,'
they'd chant like low prayer
when they were really in for it,
rubbing their hands together,
waiting to be slapped.

The young boys of Letterfrack
were a long way from home.
On sharp winter mornings
they crafted hearth rugs
for rooms they never imagined.

Such hardship could not occur
in this day and age.
Human history is an advanced course
in eternal self-improvement.

Lord, pull down the wool
from over our eyes.

Nor Was I Present

Nor was I present on the morning
you enquired how long you had left.
Later that night we watched
Leeds play Stuttgart together.
When Cantona turned the game on its head
we laughed about your preference
for strikers with raw power
like Malcolm MacDonald
and Clyde Best.

After the game was over
you pointed to the red light
on the coin-operated Salora set
at the foot of the hospital bed
and said: 'I think that thing
is using up the money
even when it's turned off.'

The late stab at thrift
was the only clue you gave
and I lacked whatever skill
it takes to tell the difference
between someone who is gravely ill
and another of the worried well.

When we were all together in Sligo,
most of us the same, monochrome,
and the county manager, Mr. P.J. McMahon
snaked across the town
in his baby-blue Mercedes,
I did not know then
what I know now.
That understated engine conveyed
the noise of low-pitched power
the capacity to hire and fire.

Replay

When I think back again
to Leeds versus Stuttgart
there was this other movement
midway through the second half
when you turned your head
away from the television set
as if sad you'd been tricked
like so often before
and were gone from the place
where outside of the game
time does not exist
where no doctor could say
what days you had left.

Yalta

There was more than I expected.
A set of toasting glasses
from his parents' wedding.
The greatcoat he was wearing
on the old Macmillan cover.
The sound of grasshoppers clicking
outside in the garden.

But, down along the boardwalk
where the lady led the lapdog
some men were executed,
their legs all chained together
and thrown into the water.
With time their bodies bloated
and stood as if to attention,
still comrades on the seabed.

Away

I saw them standing on the Rosses Point Road
where the outdoor swimming pool used to be,
this group of senior citizens
carrying multicoloured buckets,
reds, greens, blues and yellows.
I thought, *That's it, they're ga-ga,*
away with the fairies.
Turns out they were waiting for a minibus
to carry them to Bundoran
to play the fruit machines.

Fadó Fadó I, 2000, Joe Boske.

Spangle

'Dee-fence, dee-fence,' the calls
from the American basketball coach
rise above the wire mesh,
the embedded shards of brown,
green and colourless glass
in the walls of the Convent of Mercy
down onto Chapel Street
where they are not heard
by the passing Reverend Greer,
lost in the deep sleep
of an informed conscience.

Five miles away,
as the crow flies,
the Hon. Secretary of County Sligo Golf Club,
Major Mitchell Freyer,
moustache and plus fours,
is pacing the links at Rosses Point
wondering what kind of whelp
has daubed in white paint
TÁ SEÁN MAC STÍOFÁIN AN LAG ANOIS
all over Hyde Bridge.

Crossing the bridge at this moment
on his way to the post office,
Jack Muleady, the draper,
is carrying an express package
containing string vests and briefs
bound for a customer from Skreen
soon to embark on honeymoon.

Angelo Palliendo,
proprietor of the Ritz café,
is standing in the restaurant window
sellotaping a handwritten notice
declaring a tennis tournament
'open to racquet holders only'
will be held at the Merville club.

Reading from the street outside,
alert to everything, as usual,
is Henry Tamplin,
better known as 'Straightback'.
Henry opens out his arms
then moves them slowly together,
the upturned palms drawn closer
ready to serve as a clamp,
whenever he sees us approach:

'Come here to me 'til I tell ya,
would either of ye lads
like to see America?
Close your eyes for a minute
and I'll show ye America.'

My Father Meets the IMF

He was the boy with the bucket
in the corner of a damp field
shouting 'suck' to calves
hiding behind clumps of rushes.
The young man out on a Spring morning
running a pair of greyhounds
along the top of Knocknashee,
returning home in the evening
to his own concoction,
a combination of milk, bread and sugar
boiled in a saucepan.

Should, by any chance,
the moneymen venture west
and pitch their tents
in the vicinity of Sligo cemetery,
he'll surely rouse them early
and lead them up the aisle
to the headstone of Captain Edward P. Doherty,
the 'brave avenger of Abraham Lincoln'.
And, as they stand there
huddled under umbrellas
like cattle leaning into bushes
during a shower of sleet,
he'll let them know
that, sooner or later,
everyone gets nailed.

Then he'll chart the halted progress
of some rich man from the town
who ended his days, twisted,
with a round hump on his back
like a dog scraping a pot.

Woolworths

Most of those who passed
through the swing doors
had little to spend
but were drawn in
by the shiny heat,
the dark polished wood
of the floorboards,
the open-topped rectangles
of clear glass
dividing products into sections,
the pink nylon coats
of the sales assistants,
the red, clock-faced weighing machine
spitting cards of racing cars
with an arrow on the back
pointing out your own weight
to the nearest half-stone.

Opinion

I was full of opinion
when my father told me of the day
he was visiting my mother
and he was called down
to the shore at Belhavel Lake
to help retrieve a suicide.
He and some other men
carried the dead girl home
on the back of an old door.
She was pregnant.
Her boyfriend, a bank official,
was quietly transferred.

We inhabited a different world.
Civics became a school subject.
Debating was the rage.
The advantages and disadvantages
of this, that and the other.
How property had its obligations
as well as its rights.
How the moment of conception
was the inception of human life.

I thought of my father
lifting the dead girl
while I watched Fr. Paul Marx
lifting an aborted foetus
standing in a glass jar
from his canvas holdall
in the packed Latin Hall.

There was screaming and shouting.
That was the term
when the Trinity Maoists
embarked on a long march
to the province of Connacht
to embrace the peasantry.

for Paul Michael

Picnic

She remembers the day at Rosses Point,
the men lying on the grass,
their heads under the engines of cars,
hiding from the sun.
They were the family by the seaside
finding their own sand dune
facing the red, corrugated roof
of the Neptune Beachery Stores.
Following the impossible freedom
of the polo-necked, middle-aged golfers
in games stretching to Ben Bulben.
Drinking hot, sugared tea
with hardly a puff of wind
as her mother shouted,
'Isn't it a glorious day?'
to a passing perfect stranger.
With her shock at the sound
of the word 'glorious',
always a mystery, before
and the broken sadness
of their enforced joy,
they didn't know whether
to laugh or cry.

Manhunt

The birds were silent in the frost.
Every field for miles around
was trampled down
like the grass terracing
after a county final.
Soldiers, in twos and threes,
huddled around roadside fires.

Down Main Street, Ballinamore,
a boy in a Superman suit
was gazing into the window
of the Clerical Outfitters' Store
when driving slowly by,
hidden in an undertaker's coffin,
went the subject of all enquiries.

Admission

When the drinking
got completely out of hand
they brought him to the hospital.
Where do you live?
the registrar asked.
I sleep in a car
down at the Spanish Arch.
Someone turned on a light
in the back of the doctor's head.
Oh, do you own a car?
No, he answered,
but you do.

The People I Grew Up With Were Afraid

The people I grew up with were afraid.
They were alone too long in waiting rooms,
in dispensaries and in offices whose functions
they did not understand.

To buck themselves up, they thought
of lost causes, of 'Nature-boy'
O'Dea who tried to fly
from his bedroom window,
of the hunchbacked, little typist
who went roller-skating at Strandhill.
Or, they relived the last afternoon
of Benny Kirwan, pale, bald,
Protestant shop-assistant in Lydon's Drapery.
One Wednesday, the town's half-day,
he hanged himself from a tree
on the shore at Lough Gill.

And what were they afraid of? Rent
collectors, rate collectors, insurance men.
Things to do with money. But,
especially of their vengeful God.
On her deathbed, Ena Phelan prayed
that her son would cut his hair.

Sometimes they return to me.
Summer lunchtimes, colcannon
for the boys, back doors
of all the houses open, the
news blaring on the radios.
Our mother's factory pay packet
is sitting in the kitchen press
and our father, without
humour or relief, is
waiting for the sky to fall.

Player

He came to dig our road.
He had a heart-shaped
tattoo on his forearm.
He could control a ball
with left and right equally.
He said he played for Sligo Rovers.
He gave me these
passing words of advice:
'Never marry a chicken-
chested woman, son.'

Daughter

At six months,
you smiled at everyone
who looked at you
I watched your head grow steady,
the way you put fists,
then sleeves, into your mouth,
kicking at a blanket,
grabbing it,
pulling it over your face.
The first time you pointed
to something
outside of yourself
and said 'that'.

I was eighteen
walking on the grass
towards Hyde Park Corner
and this smiling group
of singing Americans.
Tans, blonde hair, perfect teeth,
all wearing white clogs
and distributing leaflets
written by Moses David
deconstructing the song
'American Pie'.

Be careful in the world.
The children of God
are nowhere as wholesome
as they seem to be.

At Vilnius everything was white.
By Aberdeen it was green. I heard birdsong.
That bird, the lark.

Irena

Her train travelled through the night
across the blacked-out countryside.
All of the names of the stations were erased.
She thought the entire region was called HOVIS.

Fifty years later,
we came upon a place,
a grove of laburnum.
The yellow flower, she said,
was growing outside the camp gates.
The Germans held a party.
The whole village was invited.
There was a band playing,
plenty to eat and drink,
music in the open air
and all the local girls
danced with the soldiers.

Rugby

Sitting with my grandmother
listening to a rugby international
relayed by Radio Éireann.
The reception comes and goes
like the wind outside.
The commentator is called McWeeney.
Cecil Pedlow is playing for Ireland,
Mike Campbell-Lamerton for Scotland.
Neither of us has ever heard such names
or so much as seen a rugby ball.
We are taking our cues
from the roars of the crowd
and the game we imagine
seems equal to any.

The Power of Verse

On darker evenings
down Mail Coach Road
lured by the bright
square box of light
boys liked to approach
Starry Dalton's filling station
and chant at Starry inside.

When they renovated the foyer
of the Silver Slipper Ballroom
the centrepiece comprised
a mural of W. B. Yeats.
Hair blown back,
pen and notebook in hand,
composing as he walked
absentmindedly along Strandhill beach.
Oblivious to the holiday makers,
the rosy-cheeked children,
mothers in polka-dot dresses,
sand castles, buckets, spades,
little windmills held in the hand,
even the sun shining.

Looking for a chase,
they'd chant at Starry inside:
'One starry night
as the moon shone bright
I saw a man out shite-ing,
well, I got a pole
and I stuck it up his hole
and I ran away like lightning.'

The Waldorf Salon

When England won the World Cup
we were dispatched
to Tommy Maher's barber shop
on Harmony Hill.

We sat in the queue
listening to men talk.
Everything was tipping along
until a row broke out
between two of Tommy's customers
over whether, or not, Nobby Stiles
was a dirty footballer.

The argument moved
from Nobby's being English
to which of the men
had taken the king's shilling.
When fists were raised
Tommy strode across the lino
in his white work coat
and parted the pair
like a boxing referee.

They were given the door.
The rest of us settled back
into the normal run of things.
Whoever sat in the barber's chair
under the glass cabinet
of shaving kits,
steel combs and styptic pencils,
got to do the talking.

Blinder

Most of the time
she had the feeling
that where she was
was not where she inhabited,
that decisions she had made
were not decisions she would make
in her real life
happening somewhere else
but without her.

The sun came out again,
windows reopened,
music rose on car radios.
She arranged to meet me
At Regent's Park zoo.
We stood in the light together
looking closely at the monkeys.

Joachim

He'd start from the corner of Castle Street at Aggie McDonagh's
sweetshop or across the road at Essex Williams, the butcher's
with the sawdust floor. He'd head down the street running
his fingers along the walls as he went, a small fellow with
dark hair combed back in a Brylcreemed lick while his mother
was alive, watered into any shape and prematurely grey when
she was gone.

He'd pass the Wood and Iron hardware store, the Mayfair café,
Keohane's bookshop, Enda Horan, chemist, Drummond Nelson
& Sons, on to William Peebles, newsagent, opposite the Lady
Erin monument.

Then he'd cross to Grattan Street and the Grosvenor Guest
House, closed for years but still displaying a TRY OUR DELICIOUS
ICES sign in the window above a drawing of two English
children, a boy and a girl, eating cones of a type never available
in Sligo.

Joachim rounded the town twice daily. He did and said most
things twice. His greeting was always half question, half
statement: 'I suppose you knew me mother. I suppose you knew
me mother?' Whenever he went to a match in the Showgrounds,
he'd take on the mood of the crowd and shout, 'Break his leg,
break his leg.' And when he met a man of the cloth he'd yell,
'Father (whatever the priest's name was). A horny man. Father
(…). A horny man.'

People laughed and said Joachim was a concert, saying such
a thing about a priest. If they were not all under ground, they
would not be laughing now.

Welcome

Five o'clock on a November evening. Standing alone by a
bus stop on Ellison Street, Castlebar. A grey day with a
cutting east wind. A man on crutches appears from around
the corner. I am stupidly surprised by the colour of his speech,
the vigour of his language: 'Those bastards down the Health
Centre, they stole the clamp of me stick, the rubber clamp.
It's useless without it,' he says, waving a crutch in the air.
He beckons to a shop across the street, 'They were here
earlier today, stealing in Heatons. The guards were called.
All from tinker town.'
I am wondering if he means Ballinrobe or Tuam when a
second voice interrupts us from behind: 'Am I north, south,
east or west? Am I north, south, east or west? I am in this
country seven days. I am staying in Doctors' Res. I am doing
gynae. I want to go to Drogheda.' There is the silence that
could be confused with appraisal before the man answers,
'You'll have to go over there to Flanelly's Bar. The fellow
behind the counter has a bus timetable.'
The doctor heads down the street and we watch as he
disappears through Flanelly's swing doors. The man with the
crutches shouts to the world in general but not to me, though
we are alone on the street: 'The bus will freeze the balls off
that lad. Not that there is a fucken bus.'

Ellen Nora Harkin
(1) After the Vacation

At 82, you touched down,
improved in a floral dress,
with your hair cut short:
'They're all getting on well in New York.
Everyone has two houses there.
I didn't get as far as Chick-argo.'

Ah, but in Chicago,
men in telephone booths
were crying into receivers,
arguing across the years,
calling their dead mothers
in homes without electricity.

Ellen Nora Harkin
(2) Devotions

Currants and raisins, your Christmas exotica
are lost in delicatessens.
The card-players are in bingo buses
on their way to singing pubs.
Most of us are living
in a town locked between
two mountains and the sea.
It is Saturday evening, still.
Tommy Maher, the barber,
is talking of football.
The hair is swept neatly in piles,
lying by the fire grate,
waiting to be burned.
Lights are going on in hallways.
Black coats, black hats, thistle hatpins
prepare for Devotions
Fr. Trench S.J. holds
the microphone like a chalice
as he speaks to the world:
'Children of Mary,
Little Crusaders of the Blessed Sacrament,
we have all come through,
though you may not know it,
a most difficult time in Catechetics'.

Balance

Ten years old, three years on
from reaching the Age of Reason,
Brother Vincent, the headmaster,
takes us for a special class.
He employs two teaching aids:
A set of weighing scales
and a box of matches.

He explains the mechanism of the scales.
The weight on one side represents our sins,
the other side, our good deeds.
He points across the schoolyard
towards the mountain of Knocknarea
and asks us to imagine
if a bird were to carry a pebble
in its beak every one hundred years
from the top of Knocknarea
and fly across St. John's school,
down Temple Street, over the cathedral
in the direction of Ben Bulben
and place the pebble on that mountain,
then, by the time Knocknarea
had been entirely transported to Ben Bulben,
eternal hell would not have even begun.

He lights the match and places it
under his downturned palm
before quickly drawing it away.
He calls for volunteers
but there are no takers.
'It is only a match on the hand,'
he says. 'Consider the pain
of your entire body
sizzling for all eternity.
Think back to the scales, boys.
Make sure the balance of your lives
is tilted in the right direction.'

John

Pass the stone soldier
and the bonesetter's house
to the field by the lake.

Good manners, you said,
was taking into account
what another is feeling.

For the funeral Mass
you asked that the priest
thank all those who came

especially the ones standing.

Dear Son

We cannot put the clock back.
Those cattlemen I knew
are a forgotten people now.
They achieved nothing except
disaster in most cases.
Your mother was the mainstay,
like the Royal Scots Express,
always running on time
and in all situations.
Everyone you think anything
about is keeping okay.
Do you suppose we were happy
once, in our own way?

Companions

I've met them in my day.
A fellow whose name I cannot remember
with lugs like Lúidín Mac Lú.
Bertie Aylott from the North Pole Road
who took the *Racing Post* and *Psychic News*.
The cranky couple in the corner
of the White Horse and Bower,
Fanny Fink and Sweetie Anthony.
The butcher ginger from Winnersh Triangle
who topped himself with a humane killer.
Matt Mulready, late of Fossett's Circus,
funniest man from my home town.
Show me your friends, my boy,
and I'll tell you who you are.

Cresting the Wave

The saddest man in Sligo
with black, ringleted hair
wore a heavy coat all summer long,
stood still for hours
in the Nazarene field
where his mother was buried.
Shadows from the narrow streets
of our town followed him.
Whenever the sun came out
or went in behind the clouds,
the change in light
terrified him.

He knelt down in Wine Street
and cried like a baby;
'You have me heart broken,
you have me heart broken.'
Tears streamed from him so freely
he became a tourist attraction
known to all and sundry
as 'Laughing Eddie'.

A day in the early seventies,
May coming into June,
a grey-haired man named Bruen
in a dark-grey pinstriped suit
came into Saint John's school
to talk about the I.D.A.
He spoke of the golden future
opening before us all.
Economics moved in cycles,
we were the crest of the wave.

Some smart fellow at the back,
Toolan from Coolbock,
shouted up at Bruen:
'Well, if that's the case, sir,
what about your brother, Eddie,
has he not heard the news?'

Bruen completely flipped;
'That delicate vessel,
he nearly broke me.
I was decent to him as any man
who ever put a hand
out through a coat.
Deep Heat, Algipan,
Sloan's Liniment, Ralgex,
Pulmo Bailly's Cough Linctus,
he was never without a tablet.
If you want to know me, son,
come and live with me.'
And forgetting all about Economics,
Bruen took up his briefcase and left.

I was talking later that day
to my special friend and confessor
The Reverend Owen MacGlone
who had high hopes at the time
I'd become a fisher of men
in Trenton diocese, New Jersey,
a place where he had lost his thumb
in an automobile accident.
The priest was in a funny mood.
He my child-ed me this and that.
All he wanted to talk about
was nocturnal emission,
what he liked to call
'Wanking Practice'.

'It has to come out some way,'
Fr. Owen said to me.
'Concerning the two brothers,
Bruen from the I.D.A. is easy.
If ever things go wallop,
he can start again in the morning
as though nothing had happened.
So far as the other fellow goes,
it's a lot more complicated
for anguish has no memory
in the mind of Laughing Eddie.'

Then he waved his hand in the air,
the one with four fingers on it.

Love Is for Life

The latest bulletin on love
declares it to be breathtakingly beautiful.
On the cover
two doves in a blue sky
are backgrounded against a scene
from the Canadian woodlands.
Fergus reads from the pamphlet
at the Catholic Marriage Advisory Centre,
'It's you two against the world,'
he tells the engaged couples.

Fergus is happily married for twenty-two years,
expert at bridging loans,
blessed with seven children.
The course tutor, his sister, Dervla
carries in thermometers and charts
to illustrate the Billings method.
When Dervla mentions the word 'mucus'
in an entirely sexual context,
the spiritual adviser, Fr. O'Carroll,
quietly leaves the room.
On a blackboard behind Dervla,
Fergus projects a map of the vagina –
It might just as easily be
the valley of the river Euphrates.

'Women are not like men,' Fergus says,
'women are like irons,
they take a while to warm up.'
'And men are not like women,' Dervla answers,
'men are like light bulbs,
they switch on and off.'
'Women like to talk a lot,' Fergus says.
'Men like to be praised,' Dervla counters.
'Next time he is digging in the garden,
wave to him from the kitchen window.'
Run Tom, Run Mary, Run Billy, Run Spot.
        RUN, RUN, RUN.

Goodnight George

'Goodnight Vienna'
was a light opera,
a trial collaboration
between Mercy girls
and Summerhill boys.

I attended every rehearsal.
The freelance director
wore a yellow cravat,
waved a cigarette holder.

Under the eyes of the nuns,
he danced all the girls
across the convent floor.

I had his measure
but he had mine.

He assigned me a role
standing centre stage
behind an apple tree.

Unseen by the audience,
I held up the prop
while couples waltzed by.

They Tell No Tales

As I think of them from afar,
the biggest bone I have to pick
with the lovely men,
the consumers of tinned grapefruit,
concerns how utterly, totally silent
our dear departed are.

She Elopes with Marc Chagall

Across fields of rotting cabbages
that nobody wanted to buy,
the girl I loved went flying
to the other end of the sky.

Up she flew —
Over the enormous satchels
of the homebound scholars;
over the disused dancehalls
and empty factories;
over the wandering dogs
in the caravan camps;
over the five upturned wheelbarrows
outside Grogans Hardware Store
on Main Street, Swords;
over the fleet of Escort vans
selling fruit, fuel and vegetables
on the Dublin–Belfast road.

When I went to the doctor, he said,
'In a week or two it'll be Easter,
the sun will shine after tea,
you'll be yourself again,
sure of who you are,
clear as a bell,
with all the time in the world
to find someone else.
In the meantime,
should that scalding sensation
in the pit of your stomach persist,
try writing some verse.'

Tra-la-la, la, la.
When it's springtime in Ireland,
the fog comes in from the sea,
the birds revive in the mornings,
the earth smells sweet under me.

At night the Rockabill foghorn
summons her back from the dead,
I remember her cheeks in blossom,
the way that she turned her head.

Easter came and went –
Despite the quack's advice,
I'm no better now
than when I began.
I torment myself
by chanting their names:
Maggie-Maggie,
Marc Chagall.

Footballers

Lost figures on chewing-gum cards.
Huge heads on tiny frames.
Mel Nurse, Albert Cheesebrough,
Ivor Allchurch, Alex Young 'the Golden Vision',
and, most coveted of all, Stan Matthews.
A skeleton in shorts, the wizard of dribble.
He made the ball talk
and we gathered bits of his life:
the rows of red-brick terraced cottages
in Hanley where he was born;
afternoons he spent lathering chins
in his father's barber shop;
his love for Betty Valence,
the coach's daughter;
in Lisbon, his favourite ground
the Stadium of Light,
all olive trees,
some seats of white marble.

By the weighbridge in Sligo,
the Gomey Adlums are having a game.
Quick flicks and delicate touches.
Mousey Sykes is there, Shifty Donlon,
Thunder Colreavy and Black Mooney.
Maestros in plastic sandals
with eyes in the backs of their heads,
on this particular patch, freed for an hour
from the awkward lunges of the well-to-do.

Stretch

Once, out of the blue,
never having remotely
touched upon the subject before,
my own father said to me,
'It was of a Saturday,
the night you were born.'

Desertion

The summer crowds have departed –
All the parasoled tricycles,
the golfers on the hill,
the old lady who sings
'Knees Up Mother Brown'
unveiling varicose veins for Americans
in the Wicklow Hotel.

The couple walking at Salthill
married quietly, out of season.
He was a civil servant,
she owned half a house.
Disharmony entered the bedroom at night,
broken glass shone on the tarmac outside.

United by day, they bypass the distasteful,
the fields of tented people,
predominance of pink
among clothes on the bushes,
the dry, unhealthy, fair hair
of the children, large rats
stirring in the reeds,
hacking the foam
of a discarded armchair.

It is a cloudy Sunday,
they are doing the promenade,
no swimmers, nothing to disturb
faint sunlight on the water,
only a wooden diving raft,
its roped matting the colour
of a bishop's beret.
Further out to sea,
framed by rungs of the raft ladder,
a tug is also leaving.

Saints

Padre Pio's secretary
is interviewed on Irish television.
He describes his former routine,
the removal twice-daily of sacred bandages,
the replacing of black mittens.

It is 1962, again.
The sun's terrible movements
across a concrete yard.
A warm-up juggler tosses eggs in the air.
The group of travelling players arrive
to present 'The Life of Maria Goretti'.
We scream when the gardener plunges
the knife in the young girl's heart
but her final, awful sighs
are accompanied by the violin music,
the classroom floor is suddenly
strewn with enormous petals.

Belhavel Lake, 1896: The Old Story

That Sunday,
father brought me down
to the Montgomery place
near Belhavel Lake
when they were all away.
It was full of furniture inside,
with pictures on the walls.

You might have heard tell
of The Belhavel Trio,
the famous Leddy Brothers.
They played all over –
London, Boston, New York.

As he lifted me up
the sun was shining.
I'd never seen pictures before.

The place was knocked soon after,
men came from the North
and carted the stones away.

'Footballer down,' she shouts
at the playpen, 'footballer down.'

But the young went away,
the Rifles and Toper,
Wild Wisdom, Mick Greaney,
what chance had they?

Ah, you're a rogue
and I'm another.
You'll hang by the rope
and I'll hang by the rubber.

Weren't that crowd badly
carting the stones away?

The rubber'll break
and I'll be saved
but you'll be hanged forever.

Boys, Oh Boys, Oh Boys.

Healing

Winter when she left,
I'd find her shape
in stains on tables
after mealtimes.
On the wet barks
and bare branches.
Running with the rain
down grey, stone walls.

By February I'd so tired
of every clump and whin,
I fled the country,
the whole dog's dinner
forever in need of a trim.

That summer I could lop
the days we spent together
as easily as dandelions
lying low along the rims
of choking city lawns.

Commuter

The life he stepped into
was never his own.
A tearing-by
of empty carriages
as the night fell.
Past dog-shit and window boxes,
he turned for home.
Little silver trains
were heartbeats on his pillow
until the silent gliding
of the Express milk float,
the table set for breakfast,
the train, again,
the woman across from him
applying make-up,
the smell of corned beef
near Clapham Junction.

Surrey Side

This morning at Quinlan Terry's
Toytown Riverside,
I saw two police frogmen,
standing in their wetsuits,
being hosed and disinfected
lest they catch Weil's disease
while diving for suicides.
The usual painting group was in session
doing clear skies over Richmond Bridge,
and an early angler
with a tinful of maggots,
bubbling like Rice Krispies.

One of Our Own

See that fellow over there,
He's a mane get.
Cut him dead.
He embezzled a lot of money,
his wife isn't well in the head.

He molested children, too, in his day.
He was assistant planning officer,
took early retirement,
was pushed out of the way.
Before he left,
he refused permission
to half the bucking country.

He was severe enough with his own.
Signs on, they fled the nest.
Not one about the place.
But who can throw the first stone?

He's not a bad fellow, really.
His bark is worse than his bite.
Behind it all, he's a nice poor devil.

I wouldn't have anything said, no,
not against Redmond McEntee,
deep down he's alright, the last word,
a gentleman from head to toe
who never did any harm to me.

In the Free World

No, we are not finally called home.
When we get out of this
particular neck of the woods,
there is nothing on the other side,
not the parents of Monsignor de Brún,
the ex-members of the Artane boys' band
or a single representative from Taiwan.

Each year we become less,
we anticipate the deaths to come
of those we truly love.
Will they be relayed by telephone
or, personally, face-to-face?
Inadvertently, from a stranger's mouth?
Once or twice, perhaps, in letters?

For the umpteenth time, a voice
on the television is saying,
'Here he is, the most powerful
man in the western world.'
And the omnipresent attaché case.
Overhead, the helicopters are whirring.
The manholes have all been checked.

I am losing contact with
even the innermost things.

The day we were released early
from Doonally infant school,
one of the teachers had gone to the well.
We walked home under trees.
The light played marvellous tricks
along the clayey path.
The sun shone through, between
the moving leaves, et cetera,
catching the puddles underneath.
Oh, to be in Donaree
with the sweetheart I once knew.
I held my sister's small hand
not wanting to reach the main road.

Camogie

Gaelic Sunday at New Eltham,
a match from home over the radio,
awkward, incongruous colours
on the women, children delving
into imported packets of Oatfield's sweets.

Back in the city of the Tribes,
the blond girl practising camogie,
bending, lifting, striking effortlessly.
At Nimmo's pier, Jenny
watching piebald horses
and imaginary Arab stallions.

The flags down for the game,
the sliotar in the air,
her face among the others,
healthy girls in their prime,
players all out of position
following a thing in flight.

Every Part of It in Rains

Though it never was my name,
he used to call me Eileen.
He'd come into reception
and deal with me alone.
'It's your special caller, girl,
the Paddy dosser.'
But I was well pleased.
The first claim I processed
was an emergency payment giro
for a homeless man.

The cow of a supervisor demanded,
'Is he kipping in our area?
If he's not kipping in our area,
then tell him to bugger off.'
He told me he was sleeping
near hand to Blackfriars Bridge
which every functionary knew
came under the caring wing
of Southwark I.L.O.,
not Battersea office at all.
It was cold November, outside.
They were sweeping up the leaves,
they were knocking down the street.

So, every second Monday,
you couldn't stop him talking;
'Boy, but time brings changes.
Things are looking up
in the old country.
There's a half-page photo
in this week's Irish Post.
One of the younger Haugheys
Is digging for gold.
Then again, do you think
it's the last throw of the dice?
No, I'll stop where I am.
There are places worse than the river.'

I looked into his face.

It was free of the town of Athy.
It was free of Gay Byrne.
It was free of Pat Kenny.
It was free of all the Smurfits.
They never entered his head.

When anxiety came to him,
it flew into his stomach.
The flits around his innards
were little birds
that put on weight
and held him down
until he could not move.

He'd sit all day in the waiting room
writing me notes I'll never forget.

Eileen – I would like Ireland for good –
My country – life in danger here
from a policeman of England –
Mr. John Brain – I left his service.

Eileen – I know Ireland very well.
Like my person. Went over it –
Know every part of it in rains.

Eileen – please excuse paper,
No money – no envelopes.
Better being a real tramp.
I will end wrong in this world.

Eileen – I lived alone in Corporation house
owned by Public Works Department.
Shaftpool Lane – my life of hell.
Metropolitan police officer no good.
A Mr. Brain – my life is hell on earth.

Eileen – I lost my father last year.
81 years old – Big loss to my person.

Eileen – I'm Irish in England since 1960.
Many works – hospitals.
I am not educated – 52 years old.
I want some kind of happiness.
Please marry me.

Eileen – I had my house –
Was wrecked even bulbs –
Wires in cooker ruined.
Hit in my eyes –
Beatings purple.

Eileen –

The last time I saw him
standing on the new pavement
outside the Golden Halibut takeaway,
he struggled to greet me
and shook my hand:
'How are you, Mrs. Brain?
And how is John?
And all the little ones?
Please send them my regards.'

If I had a heart,
he'd surely break it.
I ran through the market
of Strutton Ground,
was stopped by a wheelbarrow:
Purchased two pairs
of cotton shorts
for five pounds ninety-nine,
in a nautical design.
I'll never wear them.

Epilogue

All the old players
are falling like skittles.
The Waldorf Salon
has vanished without trace.
The town I grew up in
lives only in minds.
Its heart was torn open
by a drive-thru bypass.

biographical note

1991, Ann Costello.

Michael Gorman was born in Sligo and
educated at Summerhill College and
National University of Ireland, Galway,
where he tutored and taught for many years.

Fifty Poems is an amalgam of new and
collected work.

acknowledgements

Thanks to Mary Ruddy and Vincent Murphy
of Artisan House for their painstaking care,
attentiveness, and innovation.

To Leo Hallissey, Oliver Jennings, and
Kevin Whelan for their encouragement.

To Joe Boske and Ann Costello for
illustrations. To Connemara Community
Radio for the recording of poems. And to
my family, especially Margaret Murray,
for everything.

Acknowledgements are due to editors of
BBC Radio 4, *Everything to Play For*,
Force 10, *The Galway Review*, *The Honest
Ulsterman*, *The Irish Times*, *Krino*, *Lifelines 3*,
Lifelines New and Collected, *Paris Atlantic*,
RTÉ, *The Salmon Anthology*, *The Simon
Anthology*, *The Sunday Independent*,
The Sunday Tribune, *Voices and Poetry of
Ireland*, *Windharp: Poems of Ireland since 1916*,
and *Writing in the West*.

Published in Ireland 2019 by Artisan House Ltd.,
Letterfrack, Connemara, Co Galway, Ireland.

Editorial Director   **Mary Ruddy**
Creative Director   **Vincent Murphy**
Copy Editor   **Stan Carey**
Illustrations   **Joe Boske** and **Ann Costello**
Printing   **Imago**

Design © Artisan House Publishing, Connemara 2019
Illustrations © Joe Boske 2019 front cover, and pages 2, 8, 19
© Ann Costello 2019 page 66

ISBN **978 1 9124650 4 0**

A CIP catalogue record for this book is available
from the British Library.

Paper used in the production of this title is made from
wood grown in sustainable forests.

Books of *taste*,
Created with *passion*,
In the heart of *Connemara*

Artisan House is a publishing company creating beautifully illustrated
high-quality books and bespoke publications on a richly diverse range
of subjects including food and lifestyle, photography and the visual arts,
music and poetry.

www.artisanhouse.ie